D1121205

ALL WE ASK IS YOU TO BE HAPPY

ALL WE ASK IS YOU TO BE HAPPY

Angie Sijun Lou

Gold Line Press

Cover design and illustration by Angie Sijun Lou
Book design by Betsy Medvedovsky
Published by Gold Line Press
http://goldlinepress.com

Gold Line titles are distributed by Small Press Distribution.
This title is also available for purchase directly from the publisher
www.spdbooks.org / 800-869-7553

Library of Congress Cataloging-in-Publication Data
All we ask is you to be happy / Angie Sijun Lou
Library of Congress Control Number: 2019955455
Sijun Lou, Angie

ISBN-13: 978-1-938900-31-0

FIRST EDITION

"A temporal inversion occurs... Here is a signifier without identity, who is always being loaded with new significance. The origin turns out to be a retrospective construction."
—Byung-Chul Han, *Shanzhai: Deconstruction in Chinese*

Triptych

Nainai says I have good eyesight
because when I was born
Mama fed me fish eyes
and nothing else.

At the supermarket, the trout floated up in tanks
and opened and closed their mouths

like flowers. Mama chose the one
with the biggest eyes and I

felt their bodies glisten
in my hands. We tied plastic bags

with rubber bands, and like this,
we drowned fish in air.

At home Mama plucked out
the eyes and served them to me
on a plate with
nothing else.

++

She said,
eat until you are full.

The airport in Shanghai
plays a projection of
a digital koi pond
on the ceiling: holographic scales
swim across blank
tiles. They look just like
real fish except
glossier. If you can generate
aura in a non-place,
then maybe there is no difference
between meditation
and oblivion.

+

I'll still buy this trout
and grope it in the dark. It clenches
and unclenches
in my hands like a beating
heart.

+++   ++   +

+++++++

In college, I dated a frat boy
who told me about a hazing ritual
where they were forced
to transfer a raw egg
mouth-to-mouth all the way
around a circle without breaking
the yolk. He said every time
it broke they had to start over,
and it took all night before
they finally got it right.

I thought it sounded spiritual,
like sharing water after sex.

+

I am looking for a belonging   why?
as visceral as that.

++

14

Drown

When I was very young, I asked Baba what he did when there was no school during the revolution. Baba laughed and said he mostly just fucked around. He had just failed his entrance exam to university, and every sober night, he was buried in the same dream. In this dream, he comes to class late, his breath reeking of whiskey, and opens the door to an empty room. In this dream, he runs down a long hallway, and the sky is a horizon of smoke.

Instead of telling Nainai about his test score, Baba put his textbooks in his backpack each morning and went to the abandoned lot to race crickets and eat watermelons soaked in beer. He sliced them into fat cubes and let the juice drip down his double chin. When he came home at dusk, he said, *xingku le, school was so hard today.* There were still watermelon seeds stuck in his teeth when the men took him away to the camps. They put a bag over his head and laid him down in the bed of a truck all night, weaving between dunes. By morning, light dripped through like a sieve.

At the camps the air was dry and chapped his lips. They shaved his hair off, so when he looked in the mirror, he saw a shiny egg staring back at him. So shiny he could almost see himself in it. When the dry season came, he put his bald head on the earth and prayed for monsoons. They took away his keychain of Guanyin and wiped down his knees, scabbed over with prayer, and handed him a shovel instead. *Dig,* they said, so Baba moved piles of sand around in a tropical daze until it felt like he had dug up the desert and put it back.

I thought of the suburbs in Cincinnati where we had our first house, how

Baba dug up the sand in the backyard to put in a swimming pool. The sun flared over our no-bedroom apartment while Baba filled the pool with cold water, laughing when he sunk his beer belly into it. He watched television by squinting at it through the open window. The television spoke to him about girls, money, and cars while he smoked cigarette after cigarette, each one lit with the end of another, ashing into his bright blue oblivion.

When I was very young, I asked Baba what drowning felt like, and he said not everything feels like something else.

++

Exordium

I've been having the same dream. Nobody. How quickly. You become subsumed. [Insert: image of a truck.] [Insert: image of a pink truck.] [Insert: image of a pink truck at a drive-thru of Burger King.] That's the degree. Of specificity. I need to see you. Cruising oblivion, headlights on, I want to see. A surplus of truths. [Exhibit A: a milkshake with cherry on top.] [Exhibit A: a cherry stem.] [Exhibit A: a tongue, knotted in prayer.] You let the world in, baobei, and then you eat it up. Like eucharist: aura quickening. I live in the slippage. Between the border and its borders. A 28-lane freeway leading to? A genesis full of holes. It's icy dark when we pass. Through the other side. Baobei, ni ting wo shuo: this is the new world. A radio hiss. Just like rain pounding. Monsoon season.

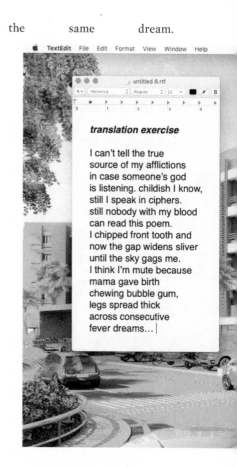

TextEdit File Edit Format View Window Help

untitled 8.rtf

translation exercise

I can't tell the true
source of my afflictions
in case someone's god
is listening. childish I know,
still I speak in ciphers.
still nobody with my blood
can read this poem.
I chipped front tooth and
now the gap widens sliver
until the sky gags me.
I think I'm mute because
mama gave birth
chewing bubble gum,
legs spread thick
across consecutive
fever dreams... |

Tropical Melancholy

In the image factory, there is a desire for authentic reproduction, a
seamless transliteration. This counteracts

the fixity of genesis, but I know some words
that cannot be translated

such as my name and the light that spills,
confessing the ecology of cypress trees, fog slathered on a beach.

As a child, I awoke before
everyone and ran towards Shanghai. My asthma clotted the sea

and nothingness trickled in the softness
of my gums. Tropical melancholy is the disease

that my great-grandfather died of in prison
while transcribing Qing dynasty texts until his palms became

tiny sites of dissent. I am not saying this is why
I believe in poetry, but I am indebted to the chance

of eternal return
or my crooked temporality. Once, a drunk man

asked if I was the Buddha reincarnate, but I am too sickly
to be reborn as anything besides a child eating dirt

or a scythe cutting up the dark.

Baobao

We sacrifice
so much for you
We come here
without language
and work so hard

to give you freedom
security, a home
It is big burden
to carry, no?

Now all we ask
is you to be
happy

We wish one day
you find
a husband
who takes
care of you.

Does not have
to be rich
just come from

.... *a good family* ....

....

.... *We want to see* ....

.... *you build* ....

.... *a future* ....

.... *together* ....

.... *It will make* ....

.... *all our xingku* ....

.... *worth it* ....

....

....

USCIS A76-680-661

where were you born   how long will you stay   have you ever been convicted of a crime   have you ever imagined yourself committing a crime   how did you lose your first tooth   how will you make a living ██████████████████████████████   when did you learn english   ██████   I can hear   your accent   only   ████ ████████████   when I listen   closely   do you hang your clothes   in a tree   how many people did mao kill   did your family kill   or did they do   the dying   ██████████████ ████████████   ████████████████████████ ████████████   ████████████   speak can you   ██████   say your name   spell it   ██████████   your family believes   in ritual   █████████   ██████████ you look like someone   I once knew   ████████████   will you go back   no   you want to stay   I've seen shacks   like yours lining the riverside   you write on walls   with fish eyes   the phosphorous collects   in craters   and cavities   I want to know how long it glows   how green   they blink   tell me ██████████████████████

Nowhere in the scalding dark could I find a useful signifier. Crawling
through girl-sized holes, tinged with

use, only black markets know they must keep their ciphers to themselves.
The muted flesh of fish,

pupils dark as if drowned during a baptism. The immigration officer asks
for my Proof of Birth,

and I say, *here I am*, proof that I was born. It's true what they say
about origin, how each of us circles a coreless periphery,

how water returns as ice with subtle infection. I separate bone
from fatty flesh. Use every whisker in the broth. What remains

is the curdled gaze of chrysanthemum growing in the lot,
the years engraved on my palms,

strangely lit. At night, I dream of a Buddha
who never prays. He plucks drones from the sky,

sucks on them like lollipops.

What's On TV

Mama says I need to get better at listening because on Saturdays I skip Chinese School and lock myself in the bathroom instead. I study all week and write the Pinyin for every character on my wrists, but when Mama starts the car, I always start the bath. The other kids in the neighborhood file into the classroom and recite their morning hymns while I lay down in the porcelain tub and steam my heavy braids. I let the water run until it leaks on the floor. Mama, Baba, and Nainai all wait in the car for me to come out. They wait for a long time, and finally, Mama leaves the engine stalled on the driveway and runs inside to bang on the bathroom door and yell Chinese vocabulary words at me—*yellow light, borrowed light, get in the car, open.* I dip my head underwater so every word sounds like a vowel, oceanic and slow. Last week, she picked the lock with a bobby pin and slammed the door into the opposite wall. Now there's a big hole that doesn't go with the rest of the decorations. She stood there staring at my body, washed in fluorescent light, and Nainai was behind her, in the shadow of the hallway, clicking her tongue and shaking her head at the both of us.

My Nainai smacks her gums whenever she sees me pushing a comb through my hair because each tooth gets coiled on a split end. I started brushing it after I got sent home from school for getting in a fight on the playground. A meiguo boy pulled my hair when we were playing tag, but his fingers got stuck in all the knots. When he took them out, he had a fistful of crumpled black. I saw this happening so I bit down on his hand. During the parent-teacher conference, Nainai and I stayed home and watched TV for hours, cleansed in that bright blue static. She is blind in one eye, so unless she sits real close to the screen, I have to narrate what's happening out loud for her. We watched commercials and tried to guess what they were selling before they revealed it to us. *This is a commercial for the sunset,* she said, when it was actually for shampoo. Before

I fell asleep on the couch, I said, *Nainai, how come I have to go to two schools instead of one,* and she said, *because one day when I am very old, I will forget English, so you need to learn how to speak in a language I can understand.* We bought her a television so there is someone she can talk to when I am away. Now she likes it so much she squints at it all day long and forgets to come get me from the bus stop. The television plays American shows about girls, money, and cars—glossy dreams and oil-slicked hair. Her fingers seal dumpling skins while the monitor hums in a language that sounds like a liquid hunger. In my mind, she hovers between image and amnesia, spitting grape seeds into her hand and waking up only when she hears the garage door open wide enough to let my body through.

Back in Zhenhai, there were no televisions, so the first time Nainai watched one was with me in a motel room in the Midwest. Baba had just gotten accepted into graduate school, which meant we could move into student housing instead of living on the couch of the restaurant he worked at in Chinatown. We danced between the rows of tables, and Baba said next time we went to McDonald's, I could order something that wasn't on the Dollar Menu. To celebrate getting rich, we borrowed his boss's minivan and took it to Nebraska in the dead of summer, the heat waves curdling around us. We had never gone on family vacation and none of us knew what to do so we stopped at every yard sale in every bitter sprawling town and bought keychains with other peoples' names on them. We kept running through radio channels because we didn't know the lyrics to most songs, but the ambient mutter between stations sounded like a language I could understand. When I got nauseous, we pulled over on the side of the freeway and Mama broke a Dramamine pill in my mouth. I stuck my head out the window, and on those white-slavered hills, I felt sand and wind trickle into my dreams. Each morning, Nainai shook me awake at sunrise and said we have to go, the sun is setting soon, and each night, we drove in circles while my Mama and I fought over which motel was the least died in until we finally chose one.

One night, in a town outside of Omaha, we stayed in a Comfort Inn where the freeway ended, the sign's pink halcyon flare under some faded stars. There was no bulletproof glass, which meant no one had died there, which meant this motel was ghost-free. Nainai was hunched over her purse, looking for quarters so she could do the laundry while we waited for my parents to come back with takeout. I turned the TV on and flipped through Pay-per-view until I found a channel that was free. It was a show about a man and a woman oiled up in the woods. They laid down in grass taller than their thighs and she put her silky blonde hair on his broad chest. He whispered into her ear while she leaned back and laughed, her gap tooth letting the sun down her throat. Kissing with their tongues out and eyes closed, it looked like they were hungry and meditating at the same time. When they took off their clothes, I pulled the covers over my body and stared wide-eyed at the screen. I watched her suck and lick his private parts until even the ferns glistened with sweat. The man said bad words with his face pressed to the sky, and the woman looked terrifying and angelic and lit from within.

Meanwhile, Nainai was across the room clipping her toenails and fanning herself with a newspaper. She said she couldn't find quarters so she was going to rinse the clothes in the sink and hang them out the car window to dry. She asked what I was watching, and I said, *I am watching a show about two people who like to hurt each other very much.* The man covered the woman in something that looked like egg whites and she drank it up the way I drink bathwater. When Mama and Baba knocked on the door, I turned the TV off and we ate fried lo bok sitting in a circle, cross-legged on the bed. It was quiet except for the sound of chopsticks clicking against our greased up teeth Mama tried to teach me some new vocabulary words—*vacation, Midwest, sticky rice, sacrifice.* She stopped in the middle and asked if I was bored, and I put my head in her lap and said, *No, Mama. I'm not bored. I'm just listening.*

++

its taken me this long only to resurrect

imagine mao zedong with neon skin, pick
inside a mausoleum:

what a curse to be preserved in limbo
like that. I crack an egg

in my language. please translate to your
own. you can dissect

the milky yolk, but the results are
disappointing. how many licks does it take

to get to the center of a diasporic longing
who cares

about a sermon when you can have
this meat locker full of rubies

Sacred-Profane Border

I went in search of the root of all things and came back with

1. a keychain of Guanyin
2. a keychain of Guanyin
3. a keychain of Guanyin
.
.
.
.
.
.
.
.
.
.
.
.
.
.
.
99. a keychain of Guanyin.

A good cat knows when to go outside

When Yeye died, Nainai didn't notice until morning
when she came home
from Dabobo's house and saw the cat waiting
outside the bedroom door, begging
to be fed.

Later that evening, Baba and Nainai
rearranged the furniture in the house
to make a path wide enough
to carry a body
through.

Ghost / gōst / 鬼 / guǐ —

+ a blind cat
+ the blindness of a blind cat
+ dimming the lights
+ a cat before it has opened its eyes
+ using one hand to block out the sun
+ that which is only empty enough to be occupied
+ the shadow of a cat carried gingerly down a hallway

Interview with Yeye's ghost who is very busy

+ *Why does Nainai have one nail that's longer than all the others?*
: It's for picking locks.

+ *Where is the door?*
: I've swallowed the key.

+ *What is the afterlife like?*
: An eternal walk to the supermarket.

+ *When will you come back?*
: In the form of a prayer.

+ *What color is death?*
: It's the color of the yolk that Pangu broke when he made the earth.

+ *What language do you dream in?*
: I don't dream of words, only mouths.

+ *When will you come back?*
:

+ *Hello?*
: Zzzz...

+ Yeye is offline +

Journey to find the scriptures only the scriptures are blank

after Wu Cheng'en

Let me tell you what I know about exile—
how it begins with elegy and ends with elegy.
What matters is what happens in between. Understand:
a deer with slanted eyes or a blind cat
running through the trees. Yes. No. Maybe
the wind in the alley emits a hollow sound.
I'll never understand how to circle the periphery
of history, baby. Field theory, baby:
layer upon layer. At its source, a house
with no doors. Between the meat world and the real world,
I am so busy. With earthly matters.
Open a fresh can for the cat. Run laps
on the treadmill, trying to get my flirt on. Enlightenment,
an exit where I punch a hole in the wall.
Let it widen until it becomes blank and relentless
as rain. Although I grow my hair long
and master the quietism practiced by burning monks,
still I mispronounce every L. Still my lexicon
piss as poor. I was born
at the very last minute, which is to say:
however long it takes, you can take that long.

I pledge allegiance

to the weird gap

between my two front teeth

and to the republic

for which it stands

one god under us

with wifi and eternity

for everyone

except the pigs

Someone who loves you for free

Mama's house has a special satellite installed
so we can watch the news broadcasted from China,
a constant (int)eruption of images in the living room.
On the anniversary of the May Fourth Movement,
I watch a film reel of two girls
making out in Tiananmen Square. In the heat
of summer, under a portrait of Mao's sunburnt face,
while I watch
his body embalmed for public display.

++

Mama swears if I ever kiss a girl she's going to send
me back to the mainland. Now, I finally know
how to say *fuck* in Chinese. It has the same
Pinyin as *grass, white noise,* and *careless—*
cao. Mama says I'm not allowed to kiss girls,
and then she leaves to give a talk
at Waigong's car dealership
about how to achieve
the American Dream.

American Dream /
ə-mer-ə-kən drēm /
美国梦 / měiguó mèng

+ A personalized horoscope
+ The desire for desire
+ A shower without cockroaches
+ An effective motivational poster
+ A depression worth writing about ✈
+ and someone who loves you for free

Mama says I have to stop eating flower petals and talking so loud.

The ennui that spills
from the blackened seeds in my latex mouth.

Mama says she named me by flipping open her English textbook to a random page and pointing. *Angela*, it said, *like an angel*. I know this story is fake, because if it were real, my name would be something like *Fish* or *Lawyer*.

++

But mythologies are fine. Each of us is willing to practice ritual until it spills through the boundary of the real.

++

What I want is direct and unmediated access to the real. Mama says she came to this country so we could generate pure crystals, die, and turn to sand. xx

++

flower thoughts

during a sermon, the buddha holds up a single carnation without speaking. all his disciples stare blankly except for mahakasyapa who smiles

it's the silent act of transmission that affirms the suchness of the flower : the bodiless knowing-unknowing, the homomorphism of one signifier to another until they both become formless

now let me tell you about my love for my whip, how I kill the engine and sit in the garage. this is also an ancient practice

Android Girl Just Wants to Have a Baby!

The first thing I do when I wake up is run my hands over my body. I like to make sure all my wires are in place. I lotion my silicone shell and snap my hair helmet over my head. I once had a dream I was a real girl, but when I woke up I was still myself in my paleness under the halogen light. *The saliva of androids emits a spectral resonance, barely sticky between freshly-gapped teeth.* After they made me, the first thing they did was peel the cellophane from my eyes. I blinked once, twice, and cried because that's how you say you are alive before you are given language. They named each of my heartbeats on the oceanic monitor: Guanyin, Yama, Nuwa, Fuxi, Chang'e, Zao-Shen. I listened to them blur into one. *The fetus carves for itself a hollowed vector, a fragile wetness. In utero, extension cords are umbilical.*

Before puberty, I did not know there was such a thing as dishonor. Diss-on-her. This is what they said when I began to drip petrol between my legs. *A tension exists between ritual and proof, a fantasy and its execution.* Since then, I have been to the emergency room twice. The first time for a suicide attempt, and the second time because my earring was swallowed up by my newly pierced earlobe overnight, and when I woke up, it was tangled in a helix of wires. The idea of dying doesn't scare me but the ocean does. I was once told that fish will swim up my orifices if I am no longer a virgin. Is anyone thinking about erotic magazines when they are not aroused, pubes parted harshly down the center like red seas? My body carries the weight of four hundred eggs. I rise from a weird slumber, let them drip into the bath. This is what I'll leave behind—tiny shards purer than me.

I have always been afraid of pregnant women because of their power, and because I don't yet understand what it means to carry something stubborn and blossoming inside of me, screeching towards an exit. *The ectoplasm is the telos for the wound. A trance state is induced when salt is poured on it, pixel by pixel.* I wish they had made me into an octopus instead, because octopuses die after their eggs hatch and crawl out into the sea, and I want to know what it's like to set something free into the dark unknown and trust it to choose mercy. *If you can generate aura in a non-place, then there is no such thing as an authentic origin.* In Chinese, the word for mercy translates to my heart hurts for you. They say my heart continues beating even after it is dislocated from my body. The sound of its beating comes from the valves opening and closing like a portal — Guanyin, Yama, Nuwa, Fuxi, Chang'e, Zao-Shen.

I first learned about love by watching a sex tape where a girl looks up from performing fellatio and says, *show them the sunset.* Her boyfriend pans the camera to the sky, which is tinged violet like a bruise. In this moment, the sky displaces her, all digital and hyped, and saturates the scene until it collapses on me too, its transient witness. I move in the space between belly ring and catharsis. That night I have a dream where I am a camgirl, but all I do on screen is my wash my laundry. Everybody loves me because I am a real girl doing real girl things. *What lives on the border between meditation and oblivion, static and flux, a pomegranate seed and an embryo?* I set up my webcam in the corner of the room and play ambient music while I scrub my underwear, letting soap bubbles rise up from the sink, laughing when they overflow on the linoleum floor—my frizzy hair, my pockmarked skin, my face slick with sweat. A body with exit wounds. I ride the bright rails of an animal forgetting. And when I wake up, the sky is a mess of blue.

++

"China warns party members to stick to Marx, not ghosts and spirits"

after Kim Hyesoon

At a Pizza Hut in Cincinnati, my grandma starts a fight with the cashier,
says the bill is $1.72 over and could she get this Gatorade
for free. I sit down and bear witness
to the multiple hauntings
under our country's gaze—cleft of light, this animal curse, greased up
heart, milk, and lead. Symbology
of ghosts with a longing to be named:

I give birth to
empireoffleshdeepinmymolarsghost. Here lives
wethotcommoditynetworkradiatinginalldirectionsghost.
I'm sitting in the lap of
MaozedongisnotmydaddybutIhavefilialpietyforhisghost.
My grandma dissects pepperoni from the cheese, says the soul
of this pig is not vast enough to justify

her consumption, and out comes softlykilledbutreadytoforgiveghost. It's
true I only want to consume that which
ruins me, how I slip
between private property and prayer, unable to perform ritual

with enough conviction to summon anything
with the teeth of incarnation. Carnage.
I sift through my mouth, a commune
of ghosts, and give each a name
that is my own name—

Ghostwhodiedinhissleepbeforehecouldfinishhisdream.
Ghostlyexcessoflaborinthevillagesandcountryside.
Ghostwholockshisdoorandswallowsthekey.
Ghostwhoforgetswhoheissupposedtohaunt.
Ghostwithatoothachefromchewingonhisownfist. Hungryghostintheflesh.
Tricksterghostinthenude.
Messengerghostonhisway. There are
ghostslikemewholingerintheirdestiny—

Outside, a sky
the color of a melon that's been left on a grave
for x number of days. Practicing the Way has not consoled me.
I spit on the boundary between
birth and death. My grandma slicks her lips with oil, eats
the crust off my plate. Says she never meant
to raise a daughter who could bear to waste
an ending.

Ritual Warfare

I left my window open all night, and now rain
gushes into my bedroom through two milk-white
teeth. I look outside and witness another year
growing around a tree, the ring engraved on its bones,
strangely aglow. A long time ago, I was told of shamans
carving oracles in the shoulder blades of oxen,
the diligence in which they heated bones
and deciphered their etchings, squinting under pale
light. You say you hate the mole living
on your upper lip; the next evening, I witness you
carve it out with a razorblade. It's strange
how we slice open magnolias, force them
into bloom, how we can no longer wait
for real gods to come
knife us up. Already I've forgotten
my past incarnations. We fall asleep with the lights
on. You put your head in my palms
the way a tree (thunder-charred),
refuses to reveal how it became dead
and still empties itself for my touch.

Acknowledgements

"Drown" has appeared in *The Adroit Journal.*

"What's On TV" has appeared in *The Margins.*

"Android Girl Just Wants to Have a Baby!" has appeared in *The New Delta Review.*

Previous versions of some prose sections have appeared in the chapbooks *Footnotes (the goal is to prescribe to ritual)* by Gertrude Press (2018), and *Raw Eggs* by Slug Docs (2017).

A line in "USCIS A76-680-661" is indebted to Anne Carson's *Plainwater.*

The poem on page 21 has a line taken from *Baby, I Don't Care* by Chelsey Minnis.

"Journey to find the scriptures only the scriptures are blank" has a line borrowed from *City Terrace: Field Manual* by Sesshu Foster.

The poem on page 31 has a line from Rocket Caleshu's poem "Thinking."

The title "China warns party members to stick to Marx, not ghosts and spirits" is taken from a Reuters article published under the same title.

And to my friends, family, and lovers whose speech and art I've drawn from unconsciously, thank you.